How to Become a Youtuber:

Your Ultimate Guide to Becoming an Influencer, Video Blogger and Making Money Online

By Dale Blake

How to Become a Youtuber:
Your Ultimate Guide to Becoming an Influencer,
Video Blogger and
Making Money Online
© Copyright 2025 Dale Blake

All Rights reserved. No part of this book may be reproduced or used in any way or form or by any means whether electronic or mechanical, this means that you cannot record or photocopy any material ideas or tips that are provided in this book.

Table of Contents

Introduction 5

Chapter 1: Choosing Your Niche 7

Chapter 2: On-Camera vs Faceless Videos 10

Chapter 3: How to Start a YouTube Channel 12

Chapter 4: Equipment Guide for Beginners 15

Chapter 5: Planning and Creating Content 19

Chapter 6: Uploading and Optimization 22

Chapter 7: How to Start a Video Blog (Vlog) 25

Chapter 8: Promoting Your Channel 29

Chapter 9: Monetization Strategies 32

Chapter 10: Analytics and Growth 34

Conclusion 37

Thank You Page 38

Introduction

YouTube flips the page completely, not the place to watch, but rather to learn, to create, and finally to thrive. YouTube allows hundreds of millions of creators to teach, entertain, and create real careers from their screens.

No matter what your passion is, make it pop on YouTube.

YouTube is your big screen launchpad no matter if education, storytelling, gaming, or writing is your niche. It is the final creative playground so that your ideas have an opportunity to become outstanding.

The book discusses all essential information on creating YouTube channels, the ways of video blogging, also inexpensive equipment choices and content ideas, including unrecognizable and visible ones, and promotion. For those who want to build their online presence, this book gives all the necessary information on how to start a video blog confidently and clearly.

To become a successful YouTuber, there is a mix of educational experiences, testing new approaches, and persevering through the process. While you should be honing your creative self-expression, your content planning skills, your brand-building skills, your audience relationships, and your analytical abilities should not be hindered in the process. Throughout this guide you will be offered practical advice alongside motivation-oriented concepts that will help you endure and improve after each video added. Every single major content creator started from a point of complete inactivity. The proper approach allows anyone to succeed.

Chapter 1: Choosing Your Niche

The most important choice for starting an efficient YouTube channel is selecting a particular niche. Your content plan and your branding elements as a whole, are all determined by this decision, as the right niche will allow you to better retain your audience.

When you choose a specific niche, you make your content more visible to its target audience since YouTube will be able to efficiently recommend it to viewers that belong to that category.

Start with Your Interests

For any successful niche creation, your passion should become the basis. Select particular topics you actually care about within your interests, for example, gaming, cooking, and fitness, and can go on to include home improvement and particular technology analysis. It is passion that makes it possible for you to come up with high-quality content on a daily basis.

With enthusiasm, you can enhance your videos, since viewers see your excitement. It's natural that you get excited about a subject and want to share it with the viewers, as your excitement for it comes out while communicating.

Market Research

Once you have selected several potential niches, you should do some market research. Study your market's performance by using Google Trends and researching keyword popularity and market competition trends with platforms like *TubeBuddy* and *VidIQ*. This research method will help you figure out your niche's popularity along with content that is already working.

As a matter of fact, watching successful YouTubers within your niche will teach you the effective strategies and the vacant opportunities for novel approaches.

Consider a Micro-Niche

By choosing a specific small subject, instead of a broad one, your channel will develop an undeniable appeal. This would help the fitness subject grow better with headings like "Home Workouts for Busy Professionals" or "Postpartum Fitness Tips."

This strategy will attract an audience looking for exactly what you provide on your channel. By specializing in micro-level topics, there will be less competition in the market, which will ensure that your audience develops stronger loyalties.

Long-Term Sustainability

Choose a specialization that you genuinely enjoy, if you can find one, because that is what will help you in the long run, stay dedicated, and be creative.

Selecting a niche you love will diminish your opportunity of professional burnout or lack of interest in the long run. Defining your niche allows you to provide your viewers with reliable benefits that commit them to consuming more content.

Why a Clear Niche Matters

It's your audience loyalty and "expert" status in your chosen area that come from a well-defined niche. A well-defined niche provides your channel with identity and direction, which allows you to develop content better and in a way that brings better results. It is important to stay true to your approach as you work across your selected niche spectrum and generally provide interesting, one-of-a-kind information to keep the viewers interested.

Defining your niche will help you find new ways to monetize the content by giving you directions in creating new content, a process that leads to the sustainable growth of your platform.

Chapter 2: On-Camera vs Faceless Videos

There is a decision that has to be made about whether you want to use on-camera or faceless videos on YouTube, and it's one that has to balance the pros and cons before you choose which will be best for you.

On-Camera Videos

Benefits: Camera videos are very effective in creating a relationship with your audience and can be used for content like vlogs, lifestyle, personal development, and educational types of content. As a result, you are able to directly communicate with your viewers instead of something more impersonal.

Challenges: If you're camera-shy, being on camera is quite intimidating. However, it needs better preparation, like good lighting, appearance, and setting.

Faceless Videos

Benefits: Faceless videos are easier to scale and give privacy. Moreover, they are quicker to make, especially when using screen recordings, animations, or voiceovers.

Challenges: All the information you can get from faceless videos isn't as personal as on-camera content. In order for viewers to stay involved, narration needs to be powerful, and the video quality needs to be high.

Hybrid Approach

If you are going to use personal content, then you might want to use on-camera videos, and if you're making tutorials or list-based content, then you can do faceless videos. It is a combination that makes you get the best of both worlds of these formats.

Key Considerations

- *Comfort Level:* If you are not comfortable on camera, faceless videos may be a better starting point.

-*Content Type:* For personal, interactive content, on-camera is great, but with faceless videos, you can get a tutorial, compilation, or informational content.

-*Time & Resources:* Faceless videos can be quicker to produce, while on-camera videos require more preparation.

Try to experiment with both formats and find out which one tells more about your topic and suits your content and style!

Chapter 3: How to Start a YouTube Channel

While it is easy to create a YouTube channel, planning carefully for each part of it will ensure greater success. Here are the step-by-step instructions to start creating your YouTube channel in order for it to be a success.

1. Create a Google Account

If you already don't have a Google account, establish one to access YouTube Studio, where you can manage your channel. YouTube Studio allows you to control your channel functions and video uploads, as well as analyze performance, with your Google account.

2. Set Up Your YouTube Channel

- Access the YouTube platform with your Google account credentials.

- Click the profile picture in the top right corner, then select 'Create a Channel.'

- You will be required to choose a channel title that is easy to remember and at the same time corresponds to your niche as well as your brand persona.

- You need to explain what content you provide, for whom, and what kind of videos to expect.

3. Brand Your Channel

- A banner design should depict the visual representation of your channel's theme. According to the recommendation, your banner should use the pixel dimensions 2560 x 1440 pixels. You can use free tools to create professional channel art with no hassle.

- Use a recognizable profile picture that represents your established brand identity.

- To increase audience participation, your banner should show your uploading schedule and social media contacts.

4. Create a Channel Trailer

- Make a 30 to 60-second video trailer introducing your content, personality, and video expectations to new channel subscribers.
- By watching this trailer, you can create a great initial connection to make viewers turn into channel subscribers.

5. Optimize Your Channel Settings

Adding the right keywords and categories for your YouTube channel settings will improve your discoverability on YouTube. YouTube's algorithm increases your content discovery potential when you pick keywords like "how to start a YouTube channel" or "vlogging tips."

6. Learn the Platform and Policies

- The first thing you should do is familiarize yourself with *Creator Academy* and the *YouTube Help Center* content, which contains necessary information about the platform, its rules and policies, and best practices.

- Knowing YouTube guidelines from the early stage helps users avoid getting strikes and monetization issues.

Key Takeaway

Establishing a proper YouTube channel and building its brand elements will set you on a path to start building the foundation of your channel for success. Consistent management, strong branding, and understanding of the regulations of the platform are the source of an attractive audience center.

Chapter 4: Equipment Guide for Beginners

Starting a YouTube channel does not require expensive equipment at the beginning of the process. When their channel hits new milestones, new YouTubers begin with basic equipment and replace it. The following sequence is a budget friendly way to start your YouTube channel.

1. Smartphone for Video Recording

Video recording features of most modern smartphone models with 1080p or 4K resolutions are excellent.

Smartphone devices come with advanced hardware sensors alongside stabilization technology that makes them suitable for vlogging and the basic content generation activities.

2. Audio Quality Matters

A budget friendly lavalier microphone is what you should get in order to enhance your audio quality.

Poor audio quality is such a major distraction to viewers that they will lose their attention, even if the visuals appear interesting.

3. Stabilization

To create a stable video footage, you will need to use either a tripod or an adjustable height phone holder.

Because of stability, your video appearance could reache professional standards.

4. Lighting

Shooting near a window will do wonders, natural light is great.

An inexpensive ring light or LED board can also come in handy if you need to do an indoor video with limited light to brighten up your face more and get rid of shadows.

5. Editing Software

There are numerous free video editing software for beginners like DaVinci Resolve, Shotcut, VN, or CapCut.

Once you have all of this covered and you prefer to acquire your skills, you can then move on to more advanced software like Adobe Premiere Pro, Final Cut Pro, or Filmora.

6. Upgrading Your Equipment

When your channel is growing, it's worth leasing a mirrorless or DSLR camera for the best quality image. For example, Canon has the M50, Sony has the ZV E10, and Panasonic has the Lumix G7. These models perform better and offers better lens options.

Pair the camera with an external microphone as well.

7. Professional Lighting

If you are filming a lot indoors, softbox lights and LED panel kits can sure bring a level of polish and professionalism to your filming that will be worth the investment.

These lighting setups ensure that each shot has consistent brightness and color temperature.

8. Faceless Content Creation

Creators who do not want to appear on camera can use screen recording tools like *OBS Studio* or *Camtasia*.

Moreover, you can easily add voiceovers via text to speech tool or via a USB microphone to create tutorials, software walkthroughs or any gaming content.

9. Thumbnails and Animation Tools

You can use free tools like *Canva* for creating thumbnails, and *Doodly* or *Animaker* for creating animated content; free stock footage for your audio visual online courses can be found at *Pexels*, *Pixabay* etc.

The Key Takeaway

Start with what you have. Keep your creativity within the budget, not the other way around. Focus on producing content, process, and your audience. It will improve your equipment as you grow.

If you want to start now with the bare minimum of equipment and grow from there, you'll see progress for the love of it or for money: good lighting, clear audio, stable footage, and engaging content.

Chapter 5: Planning and Creating Content

Just like any other successful business, to have a successful YouTube channel that you'll want to stick to, you need to plan and be a bit technical. This is a guide on how to set a strong foundation.

1. Brainstorm Video Ideas

- You ought to align the content with your niche and your target audience's interests.

- This means you would include tutorials, product reviews, challenges, behind-the-scenes, storytime, reaction videos, etc, along with educational explainers.

- This keeps your channel fresh and fascinating with all types of content material.

2. Create a Content Calendar

- Get a plan and schedule of uploads to maintain consistency.

- Select a frequency and stick to it. Trust is built by consistency, and it keeps viewers coming back.

- Stay ahead of your schedule. Batch record multiple videos at once to easily upload them later.

3. Script Your Videos

- Having clear and engaging content is what every blogger needs, and a well-structured script will help you achieve that.

- The first 5–10 seconds of the video should have a strong hook to grab attention.

- Have a clear introduction: firstly, who you are, secondly, what the video is about, and thirdly, why it matters.

- Split the main content into sections with soft passages.

- Wind it up with a CTA: Mention likers, commenters, shareables, and subscribables. Link to other related videos to engage them more.

4. Filming Quality

- Format your videos In landscape mode.

- Clean the camera lens to avoid blurry footage.

- Filming in a rather controlled environment so that background noise does not corrupt the film.

- You should use proper lighting. Natural light is best, but if not available, use soft, diffused lighting sources like ring lights.

- Try to avoid harsh shadows.

5. Editing Your Video

- Trim the content that is not needed at all to have a smooth flow.

- Also, you can add background music or sound effects to give a mood to your video without being loud enough to overpower the voice.

- Also, include transitions between scenes to make the video more professional.

- Use caption for accessibility and for users who are watching without sound.

6. Branding Your Channel

- Add your logo and watermark, as well as a branded intro and outro.

- You also need to be consistent on the colors and fonts so as to reinforce your channel's identity.

- End screens and cards should show other videos, playlists, or your website.

Putting together creativity, careful planning, high-quality filming, and professional editing will ensure that you are on your way to creating a YouTube channel that will attract and keep viewers.

Chapter 6: Uploading and Optimization

When your video is edited and ready, you will need to optimize it for YouTube to be found and engaged with. Here is how to make sure your video will perform well on the platform:

1. Upload Your Video to YouTube Studio

Go to YouTube Studio, click 'Upload Video,' and select and upload your file. Once you upload your video, you will be set to the settings page to adjust your video.

2. Write a Keyword-Rich Title

It should also be the title that would grab people's attention and reflect the content of the video. Start off with relevant keywords to make it searchable. It's important to avoid clickbait. Clickbait is a direct killer of viewer retention.

3. Write a Compelling Video Description

Create a summary of the video content with relevant keywords. Include social media links to the video, CTAs like asking for likes or comments, and timestamps for long videos.

You can also include links to videos that are related to the one you are sharing.

4. Use Relevant Tags and Categories

Use a mix of broad and specific tags that the content is relevant to. Select the relevant category to make your video appear in searches that are relevant.

5. Design and Upload a Custom Thumbnail

The thumbnail has to be visually striking. High-quality images, legible text, and contrasting colors are all highly useful qualities that will help ensure higher engagement for your videos. Canva is a tool that can help you easily create professional thumbnails.

6. Optimize for SEO

Additionally, you want to include your target keywords in your title, description, tags, and even closed captions so that they can be found. Including relevant hashtags for your video will increase the video's reach.

7. End Screens and Info Cards for Viewer Engagement

End screens and info cards can be used to direct viewers towards another content or ask visitors to subscribe. These features assist in keeping the viewers attracted, and hence, increasing channel growth.

8. Analyze Performance and Adjust

In YouTube Analytics, you must monitor the video's performance. Track the metrics CTR, watch time, and audience retention, and change according to the data to improve future videos.

Following these guidelines, you can transform your content, helping it reach a wider audience while garnering high engagement on YouTube.

Chapter 7: How to Start a Video Blog (Vlog)

Vlogging is simply video blogging, where a person records a moment in life, a day in the life, an adventure, or their opinion through video. This genre is well known on YouTube and gives the creators an opportunity to share a piece of their real life with their audience.

1. Why Vlogging?

Vlogging helps in building a closer relationship with your audience. It offers viewers the chance to connect with your personality and create a loyal, interactive community.

2. Finding Your Vlogging Niche

A targeted audience is attracted to a specific niche. Popular niches include:

- *Lifestyle:* Daily routines and personal experiences

- *Travel:* Adventures and exploration

- *Fitness & Health:* Workout routines and health tips

- *Beauty & Fashion:* Makeup tutorials and fashion advice

- *Food & Cooking:* Recipes, restaurant reviews, and cooking tips

3. Creating Compelling Vlogs

- *Be Genuine:* Authenticity is key. It's a matter of showing real life through your challenges and your personal experiences so that viewers connect with the content on a more personal level.

- *Plan, but Stay Flexible:* Ensure that you cover key moments, but leave some room for spontaneous content.

- *Tell a Story:* Keep your vlog's beginning, middle, and end engaging by structuring your vlog.

4. Engaging Your Audience

- *Ask Questions:* Ask about your audience's experience of something.

- *Respond to Comments:* By responding to comments in the comment section; you build relationships.

- *Incorporate Feedback:* Improve future videos from the suggestions of the viewers.

5. Vlogging Locations and Shots

- Vlog in Different Places: Vlog from different locations so that the content does not get dull.

- Post wide-angle shots, close-ups, and B-roll footage for visual interest.

- Use a walk or gimbal with your camera to have lively footage.

6. Vlogging Gear and Equipment

- You can improve footage quality by investing in a GoPro, a DJI Osmo, or a smartphone.

- Gimbals and Stabilizers: You'll need these to get smooth footage when you move.

- A portable mic will provide clear audio.

- Softboxes or ring lights will provide much better visual clarity in low light.

7. Editing and Post-Production

- *Use Mobile Apps:* You can do quick edits on the go by using apps like *iMovie* or *Adobe Premiere Rush*.

- *Music and Sound Effects:* Sound effects can be used to highlight specific occasions, and background music is also used as an audio flavour.

- *Transitions and B-Roll:* You can use these to ensure that the video is smooth and interesting to the eye.

8. Consistency and Growth

- *Maintain Consistent Uploads:* Maintaining consistency when uploading content is important so as not to bore your audience.

- *Track Analytics:* Change your content as per your YouTube analytics.

- *Partner:* Working with other vloggers will allow you to put your channel in front of a new audience.

There's no doubt in the fact that vlogging is a long term thing but with consistency, it pays off in the end both for your personal satisfaction and professional achievements.

Chapter 8: Promoting Your Channel

The truth is that great content is just one part of success; the second ingredient is promoting your YouTube channel in order to attract new viewers and grow your subscriber base. This is how you can do the promotion of your videos most effectively.

1. Social Media Promotion

Share your videos on a platform where people can see them, such as TikTok, Instagram, Twitter, and Facebook. Repurposed content, such as short clips and teasers, is great for generating interest.

- Post stories, reels, and feeds on Instagram.

- Share short, attention-grabbing clips on TikTok.

- Post clips of your content and be active in relevant groups on Facebook & Twitter.

2. Leverage YouTube Shorts

Create a clip from your main videos and make short but engaging videos (less than 60 seconds). Join trends, and ask viewers to click through to your full videos.

3. Collaborate with Other Creators

To increase your reach you can colab with other creators in your niche. Reach the audiences on their channels by recording co-host videos, shout-outs, or being a guest.

4. Community Engagement

Although it may seem redundant at this point, building a loyal community is crucial. Engage with your audience, reply to comments, post on the community, host live Q&A, or stream.

5. Embed Videos on Blogs and Websites

Write guest posts and upload your videos to blogs or websites that are relevant to your audience. Video marketing increases the exposure of the video and improves SEO.

6. Email Marketing

Build an email list and use it to send out your latest videos in your newsletter. Consequently, you ensure your subscribers get informed and engaged.

7. Share in Forums and Communities

Share your videos in the specific Reddit, Quora, or niche forums. You can get incredible reach if you are able to target your relevant audience on these platforms.

8. Paid Advertising

Finally, use YouTube or social media ads to drive your videos to a larger and more qualified audience. Ads can boost visibility quickly.

9. Hashtags and SEO

Make sure to use appropriate hashtags and have the best title, description, and tags for SEO. It will help your videos appear and become visible.

10. Consistency and Branding

If your channel is consistent in uploading, branding (logo, banner, video style), etc., you will retain viewers and grow your channel. Make sure to always keep to a timetable so that your audience is always up to date.

Chapter 9: Monetization Strategies

Once you qualify (or reach the threshold) for the YouTube Partner Program (1000 subscribers + 4000 watch hours), you start earning from ads. However, for growing channels, there are other ways to monetize, too.

Affiliate Marketing

Link affiliate links to your video descriptions to promote products that fit within your niche. Most of the affiliate programs, including *Amazon Associates* or *ShareASale*, will pay you on a commission basis.

Sponsorships

Since your audience will be growing, it can attract brands that may sponsor your content. They can be product mentions to full dedicated videos. However, there should be transparency with your audience.

Selling Digital Products

Sell eBooks, online courses, or other digital products. Such entities have low overhead, and they can generate passive income.

Crowdfunding

Use platforms like *Patreon* or *Buy Me a Coffee* to receive support from your audience in exchange for exclusive content or bonuses.

Merchandising

You can sell custom merchandise such as T-shirts or mugs through *Teespring* or *Merch by Amazon*. These platforms also take care of printing and shipping.

Paid Reviews and Collaborations

Earn by reviewing products or collaborating with brands. In order to keep the trust of your audience, always keep it authentic.

Diversifying Income Streams

Combine these strategies to create different money-making streams so that you have plenty of streams of income that will keep you financially stable and making money on a constant basis.

Continuous content and monetization will make your channel a profitable business.

Chapter 10: Analytics and Growth

YouTube Studio is indispensable in tracking your channel's performance. Click-through rate (CTR), average view duration, watch time, subscriber growth, traffic sources, etc., are the metrics based on which you can figure out what works and what needs fixing.

Tracking Key Metrics

Key metrics should be monitored to evaluate the success of the content. CTR is the measure of how well your titles and thumbnails catch attention. Try to improve CTR if it is low. Video engagement is measured in terms of average view duration, and if people are dropping off early, the pacing may not be good or the video may not have a strong start.

Overall channel health is measured by watch time and subscriber growth. Traffic sources tell you in which places views are coming from (for example, search, suggested videos, social media, etc.).

Making Data-Driven Decisions

Refine the strategy using analytics. If you do well in terms of certain videos, then keep an eye on what made them well, content type, length, thumbnail, etc. For a video that doesn't perform, check audience retention to spot where interest faded and adjust. To find what works best, experiment with content formats and video lengths.

Consistency and Long-Term Growth

It is the consistency that matters for long-term growth. A loyal audience is built with regular uploads. Use a content calendar to keep yourself on track and to keep from working at breakneck speed.

Always provide value to whoever it is that you're speaking to. Ask yourself some tough questions: Am I solving any problems? Are they being entertained? Optimize your videos' titles, descriptions, and tags employing SEO practice, which will position your videos in a better light.

Investing in Growth

Keep updated about the trends, changes on the platform, and shifts in the industry. To know more, subscribe to YouTube's official channels and creator communities. When you grow your channel, invest in better equipment and acquire more knowledge in editing, branding, and marketing to compete.

It takes time and effort to build up a successful YouTube channel. With analytics, consistency, and proper evolution of trends, you can have long-term success.

Conclusion

Starting a YouTube channel is a fulfilling journey, and there is no doubt about it. To start a successful YouTube channel, you will need creativity, consistency, and authenticity. Also, a way to grow your channel is by promising to be true to yourself, making good content, and maintaining engagement with your audience.

Remember! Every single YouTuber had 0 subscribers at the start, and it simply takes time to learn and get better at what you are doing. Nevertheless, if you hold your breath and start this now, you can etch your passions onto the big screen and reach out to people, while your creativity might turn into an income source.

Thank You Page

I want to personally thank you for reading my book. I hope you found information in this book useful and I would be very grateful if you could leave your honest review about this book. I certainly want to thank you in advance for doing this.

www.ingramcontent.com/pod-product-compliance
Lightning Source LLC
LaVergne TN
LVHW010419070526
838199LV00064B/5353